Series 633

*Here is another Ladybird book which will keep children happily occupied for many hours. All materials needed are simple, inexpensive and readily available.*

# TOYS AND GAMES TO MAKE

by JAMES WEBSTER

with illustrations by ROBERT AYTON

Publishers: Ladybird Books Ltd . Loughborough
© Ladybird Books Ltd (formerly Wills & Hepworth Ltd) 1966
*Printed in England*

# FURNITURE FROM EMPTY MATCH-BOXES

You will need:

> *Some empty match-boxes*
> *A few paper-fasteners*
> *Bits of coloured cloth or paper*
> *Silver-paper*
> *Some safety-matches*
> *Scissors and glue*

Match-boxes are ideal for making model furniture because they have ready-made drawers which will really open and shut.

Glue four, six or eight boxes together, push paper-fasteners through their drawers, cover with a strip of cloth or paper—and you have a little chest of drawers.

With a box glued in the middle between the other drawers, a chest of drawers can become a desk. And if the bottom of a match-box tray is covered with silver-paper (to make a mirror) and glued to the top—you have a dressing table.

Beds and chairs are easier still, as you can see from the picture. Glue safety-matches into the boxes for legs. Cut up some bits of cloth for blankets and covers. You can even make a television set!

4

7214 0126 0

# BLOWING BUBBLES

You will need:

*A piece of thin wire*
*Some pieces of left-over soap*
*Some glycerine*

Leave the pieces of soap overnight in half-a-cup of water. If there is any glycerine in the house, add one teaspoonful to your soapy water; this will help to make even better bubbles.

Bend the wire into a circle round a stick or the handle of a wooden spoon, twisting the ends of the wire together as shown.

Dip the wire circle into the soap mixture and blow gently. You should see a beautiful stream of bubbles coming from the wire.

# A BOX GUITAR

You will need:

*A strong cardboard box*
*Half a cork*
*Elastic bands*
*A penknife and scissors*

Make the body of the guitar by cutting a hole about two inches from one end of the lid. Mark lines half-an-inch apart from the hole to the other end of the box as shown.

Cut a cork down the middle, stretch an elastic band tightly over the box and then slide the half cork beneath it. From a small piece of card make a triangular 'plectrum' with which to pluck the strings. You are now ready to play your guitar.

You will find that you can soon play a tune by pressing your finger on the correct lines and plucking the elastic at the same time. You can have fun using more than one elastic band.

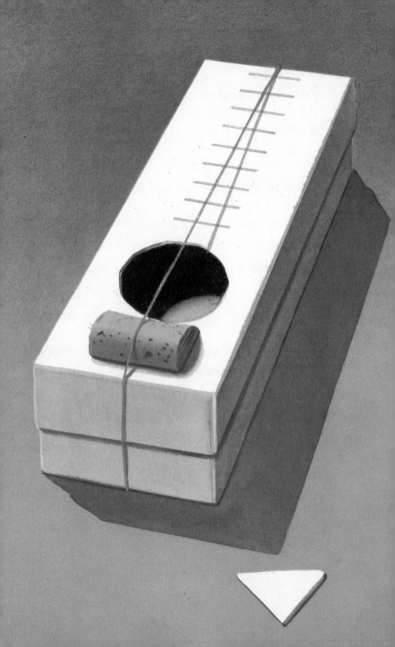

# A TELEPHONE

You will need:

*Two empty round tins*
*A long piece of string*
*A hammer and a nail*

Golden syrup tins are just right for this telephone, but you will need to wash them out well before starting work!

Make a small hole in the centre of the bottom of each tin, using the hammer and nail. Thread one end of the string through the bottom of one of the tins, and tie a knot at the end of the string inside the tin. Then do this with the other end of the string and using the other tin.

You will need a friend to help make your telephone work, as the string between the tins must be pulled tight. One of you can speak into a tin as the other listens, and you will be able to speak to one another as far apart as the string will reach.

# A KNITTING-MACHINE

You will need:

*A cotton-reel*
*Four small nails*
*A hammer*
*Some wool*
*A pointed match-stick or a hairpin*

To make your knitting-machine, hammer the four small nails into the top of the cotton-reel as shown, leaving slightly less than half-an-inch of each nail sticking out. You are now ready to knit.

Thread the wool past the nails, down through the centre of the reel until it projects about four inches at the opposite end. Hold this end of the wool firmly while you wind the wool from the ball twice right round the four nails, taking care to keep the two strands well apart.

Beginning at any nail, use your hairpin or match-stick to lift the bottom loop of wool over the top one and right over the top of the nail. Do this with the wool on the other nails. Then wind another loop of wool right round the nails and repeat the lifting process. Do this again and again—occasionally giving a gentle tug at the piece of wool protruding from the hole at the opposite end. You will soon find a 'tube' of knitting coming out of the bottom of the reel.

When long enough, this tube can be wound round and round and stitched to make a table mat, or made into reins for a baby brother or sister.

# A SPINNING SNAKE

You will need:

*A piece of silver kitchen foil*
*A knitting-needle with a point at both ends*
*An elastic band*
*A night-light*
*An old tray*
*Scissors*

Use a jam-jar to mark out a circle on the foil, and then cut a spiral snake out of this circle. Attach the knitting-needle to the side of the night-light with the elastic band.

Put the night-light on the old tray, and balance the head of the snake on the top of the needle. Bend the snake's head a little to stop it falling off. When the night-light is lit, the snake will start to spin.

If you have no night-light, thread a piece of cotton through the snake's head and dangle it over a radiator or table lamp.

# A MAGNET FISHING GAME

You will need:

*A magnet*
*A cane*
*Some white paper, and paints*
*Scissors, pins and paper-clips*

On white paper, draw about twelve fishes of varying sizes from about two inches to five inches, preferably with more of the smaller than the larger ones. Paint them with bright colours and cut them out. Fasten paper-clips to the large fish, and pins to the smaller ones. Pencil a different number on the back of each fish.

Tie about four feet of thin string to a cane, and the magnet on the end of the string. A cheap magnet can be bought from the ironmonger.

Spread out the fishes in a circle behind a chair or on the bottom of a box so that you are not able to see them when fishing. Now you can start your Angling Competition.

Take turns to lower the magnet behind the chair or into the box, and, after it has touched bottom, lift the rod and see if you have made a catch. When all the fishes have been caught, add up the numbers on the backs of your catches to see who has won.

# MINIATURE SKITTLES

You will need:

*Some corks*
*Plasticine*
*White paper*
*Marbles*
*A cardboard tube*
*Some one-inch nails*
*Paste or glue and gummed tape*

First make the skittle-men. You can make as many as you wish, and it is fun making them.

Push a one-inch nail halfway into the end of each cork, and over the nail press a ball of plasticine. Then make a small ball for the nose, two small balls pressed closely for the ears, and a larger ball pressed flat for the cap of each man. Eyes, eyebrows and mouth can be marked with a sharpened match-stick.

Glue white paper round each cork, and paint the bodies of your skittle-men in any colours you wish, but mark each one with a number.

The cardboard middle of a toilet roll is excellent for the shute down which you will roll your marbles to knock down the skittle-men, or you can make one with paper fastened with gummed tape. Fix it to the match-box as shown.

Drop each of your five marbles down the shute, aiming at the skittle-men with the biggest numbers. Remember to arrange the skittle-men so that there is enough space for a marble to pass between them.

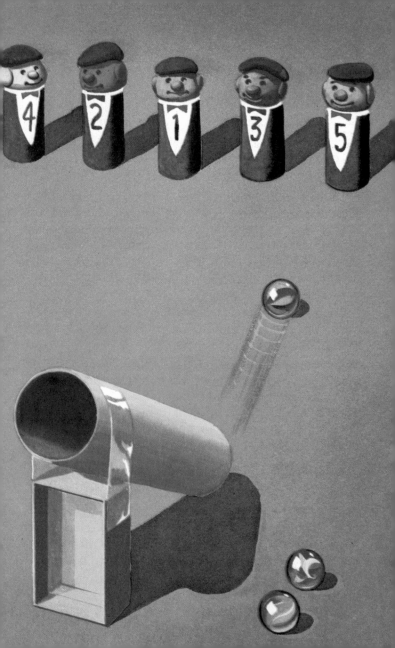

# A DANCING DOLL

You will need:

| | |
|---|---|
| *11 cotton-reels* | *Some string and wool* |
| *6 corks* | *Some beads, scissors* |
| *Some elastic bands* | *and a metal skewer* |

Choose the largest reel to make the head, and paint in the face. Cut some strands of wool and tie them together at one end: this will make the hair.

Take the cork which is to be the neck, and make a hole right down the centre with a skewer. Do the same with the cork that will form the shoulders, but also make a hole through the side of this cork. For the hands, make a hole through the sides of two more corks. For the feet, the holes need to be about half-an-inch from the ends of two more corks.

Loop some elastic bands together to make three cords, one of them about six inches long and the other two about a foot long.

Tie a bead on the end of the six inch elastic cord, and thread on a cork hand, two reels, the centre shoulder cork, two more reels and the other hand. Finish off with a bead. To get the elastic cord tight enough once you have threaded it through, you may need to shorten it by removing a band or two.

Make two legs in the same way, and thread both elastic cords up through the two reels which form the body. Now add the arms, the remaining cork for the neck and then the head. Thread the elastic cord through the centre of the tied bunch of wool (which can now be glued to the top of the head), and join it to a length of string. Jerk this up and down to make your doll dance. You can do this to music.

# A BALANCING MAN

You will need:

*Two knitting-needles*
*Two nails*
*A cork and some plasticine*

Make the man by pushing a nail into the cork for the leg on which he will balance. Put another nail in for the other leg—but at a different angle. Paint a face and some hair on the cork, and you can even cut out a circle of paper for a hat-brim.

Now push a knitting-needle 'arm' firmly into each side of the cork so that they both slope downwards. Put some plasticine at the ends for 'hands' and to act as weights.

Your balancing man should now be able to stand on the top of a bottle, or even on the back of a chair or on a tight clothes line. You may need to add some plasticine to one hand or the other, or alter the position of the arms a little, to help him get his correct balance. Two balancing men look even funnier.

# A WORKING TRACTOR

You will need:

*A cotton-reel*
*An elastic band*
*A small piece of candle*
*Two used safety matches*
*Two drawing-pins and a penknife*

This little tractor will creep about on its own, and climb things in its path.

Cut some notches in the rims of the reel so that the tractor will be able to get a good grip. Cut off about half-an-inch of candle and pull out the wick, making the hole larger with the small blade of a penknife and turning the blade round and round. Now cut a slot across one end of the piece of candle, just deep enough to take a match.

Push the elastic band through the cotton-reel and the piece of candle, and slip a match through each end of the band to hold it in place. If your elastic band is rather short, pull it through with a piece of string.

Now push the match at the candle end into the slot which you cut for it, letting it stick out as far as it can at one side. Now break off the other match and hold the remaining piece in position with a drawing-pin at each side. To wind up your tractor, turn the long match round and round with your finger. Place it on some rough ground and watch it climb.

# A TANK

You will need:

*Two empty date boxes*
*An empty chocolate box—or any of a suitable size*
*An empty cigarette-packet*
*A round tooth-paste tin and the cap from an old tube*
*Two elastic bands and four cotton-reels*
*Corrugated paper*
*Metal skewer*
*Glue and paint*

Cover the sides of the date boxes with strips of corrugated paper to form the tank 'tracks'. Glue in position.

Glue the lid on to the back of the chocolate box, and make two small holes about two inches from each end and half-an-inch from the edge. Slip an elastic band through each hole, and in each case stop the end being pulled through by inserting a match-stick. Now thread each band through two cotton-reels, pulling the bands through the other holes and securing with match-sticks. The result will be a springy 'axle' for your tank.

Glue the date boxes to the sides of the chocolate box lid, concealing the match-sticks. Bore a hole through the cigarette-packet 'turret', and glue the skewer gun (with the tooth-paste cap on the end) into position. Glue the tin 'hatch' on top of the turret, and add a match-stick for a machine gun. An upright match-stick could be an aerial. Now you can paint your tank with camouflage colours.

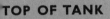

**UNDERSIDE OF TANK**

**TOP OF TANK**

# A MOTOR YACHT

You will need:

*Half a wooden clothes-peg*
*A paper-clip*
*Some used safety matches*
*Some cotton*
*A plastic bowl and a magnet*

Round off the ends of the half peg into the bows and stern of your yacht. You can do this with a penknife and sandpaper, or simply by rubbing it against some concrete. A little floor polish will give it a finished appearance.

Bend the paper-clip into the shape of a 'T', and bind it to the bottom of the yacht with the cotton. For the mast, glue a match upright in the slot on the deck, and two or three more side-by-side and flat to form the cabin. You should use a waterproof glue like balsa cement, but a drop of old nail varnish will do.

Fill a plastic bowl with just enough water to let the paper-clip clear the bottom, and support the bowl on two boxes or some books (either underneath the bottom or the rim). Now move the magnet underneath the bowl, and your yacht will sail wherever you wish. If the magnet is a powerful one, you may need to add a little more water to prevent the yacht diving!

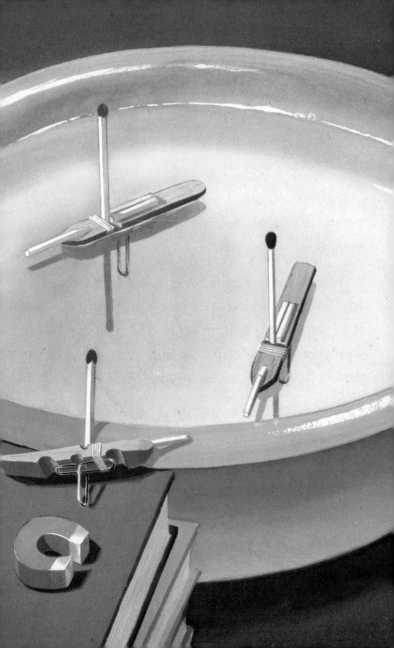

# A POWERFUL PADDLE-STEAMER

You will need:
*Two empty match-boxes*
*Three used safety matches*
*An elastic band*
*A cork*
*Scissors and glue*

The first steamers were driven by paddles, not propellors. This model has one paddle at the back and will move along very quickly.

Wedge a match-stick firmly in each side of the match-box, between the box and the tray. The match-sticks need to be pointing slightly downwards. Then stretch an elastic band over the ends of the matches. You will probably need to double over the band to shorten it.

Cut a 'paddle' from the end of the other match-box tray, and slip this between the strands of the elastic band. Glue the cork funnel and the match-stick mast in place. Your paddle-steamer is now ready for launching.

Twirl the paddle round and round so as to wind up the elastic band, place your steamer at one end of the bath of water—and away she will go!

# A CARGO BOAT

You will need:

*The top or bottom of a date-box*
*A cigarette-packet—preferably the 'flip-top' kind*
*A match-box*
*Two corks*
*Four match-sticks*
*Some white paper*
*Paste and glue*

Paste a strip of paper around a cigarette-packet, and also around a match-box and a piece of cork. Then paint them as in the illustration.

Glue the cigarette-packet inside and at one end of the date-box, and then the match-box on top. Then glue the cork (as a funnel) on top of that. Now your cargo ship is beginning to take shape.

Glue the four matches into position as shown. To make the lifeboats, cut a cork lengthways through the middle, and cut a point at each end of both pieces. They can be painted white, and glued into position between the upright match-sticks.

It is a good idea to paint the date-box black and to use house paint. This is water proof, and will enable you to float your ship on your nearest paddling pool. Indoors, you can have fun making your boat carry cargo around the room. If you make the crane on page 34, you can use it for loading and unloading.

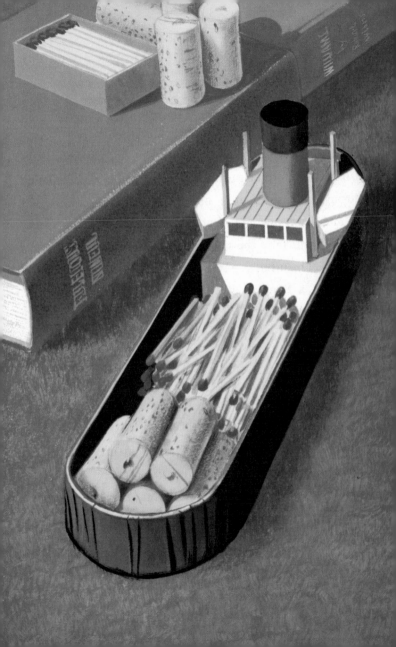

# A REVOLVING CRANE

You will need:

*An empty tin*
*A piece of wood, a ruler and a match-box*
*Gummed tape and some strong thread*
*Two paper-clips, a small nail and some glue*

Nail the lid of the tin upside down on the wood, just firmly enough to be turned around smoothly. Make holes through the sides of a match-box, about a quarter-of an-inch from one end. Put the open end of the tin inside the lid, and tape the match-box to the side of the tin as shown. Open out a paper-clip and then bend it into the shape of a handle with a long shaft, pushing the shaft through the holes in the match-box.

Cut a small notch in both ends of the ruler, and tape it over the end of the tin and with one end projecting about an inch over the match-box. Make a slip-knot round the shaft of the winding handle inside the match-box, draw it tight and then put on a spot of glue to secure.

Make a hook from the other paper-clip and tie it to the other end of the thread. Pass the thread through the notches in the ruler—and you are ready to wind up objects from the floor, swivelling the crane when necessary.

You may need a plasticine weight above the hook to make the thread run smoothly.

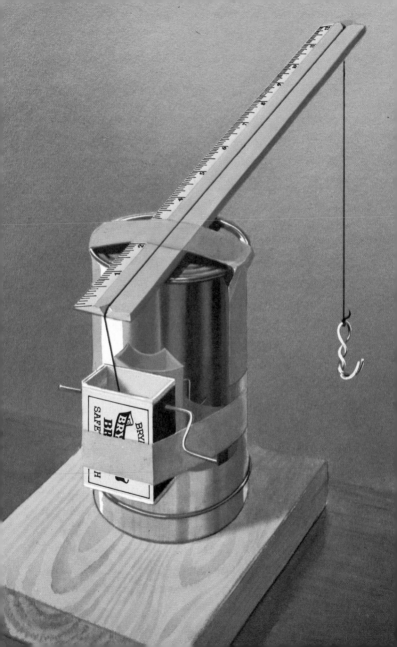

# A MAGIC WALLET

You will need:

> Two pieces of fairly stiff white card, each about 3 ins.
> by 4½ ins.
> Two pieces of ribbon, each about 14 ins.
> A picture or photograph
> Scissors and glue

Lay the two cards side-by-side on the table as in Fig. 1, and with the best surfaces downwards. Glue down the ends of the ribbons as shown, and wait until dry. When the ribbons are firmly attached, pass each ribbon under the left hand card and then over the right hand card as shown in Fig. 2.

Now pass the ribbons under the right hand card as in Fig. 3, and pull gently on them until the edges of the cards are fairly close together as shown. Glue down the ribbons in the positions shown, and trim off any unwanted ribbon.

Your magic wallet is now ready, but you can improve its looks by pasting pieces of wallpaper over the outside covers, hiding the stuck-down ends of the ribbons.

You will find that you can open this wallet from either side. Open your wallet from one side and place a picture or photograph under the ribbons on the left or right. Close the wallet and then open it from the other side. You will find that the picture has magically changed its position. Try it on your friends—they will be amazed.

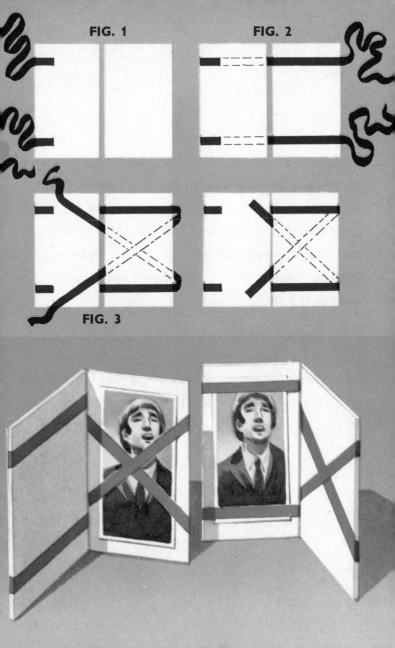

FIG. 1

FIG. 2

FIG. 3

# A BOOMERANG

You will need:

*A strong piece of card*
*A pencil and ruler*
*A penknife*

Measure out or trace the boomerang in the picture on to the card, and then cut out this shape with a penknife. You could ask one of your parents to cut it out with a razor blade. Do not use scissors, as these are likely to make the cardboard curl, and this will stop the boomerang from working properly. Make sure all the edges are smooth and flat.

To 'throw' your boomerang, place it as shown on the edge of a cardboard box or a book, and flick it forward with a stick or pencil. Remember, it *must* be perfectly smooth and flat to fly correctly and come whirling back to you.

$3\frac{1}{4}''$

$3\frac{3}{4}''$

# A MOVING PICTURE

You will need:

*A piece of paper about 10 ins. by 4 ins.*
*A long pencil*
*A pen and black ink or paint*
*Some tracing paper*

Fold your paper in half as shown. Now carefully trace the dog in our picture, including both positions of his tail. Rub the side of the pencil all over the back of your tracing. Unfold your paper, and with the fold at the top make your tracing on to the lower half of the paper and in about the position shown. On this drawing, show the tail bent to the left only. Now ink or paint in.

When dry, fold the top half over your drawing and hold flat against a window pane, when you will be able to see your first drawing. Hold in this position while you trace your first drawing . . . but without a tail. Now ink in or paint this second drawing—*adding a tail bent over to the right*.

Take a long pencil and roll the top flap over it as far as it will go. Hold the paper as shown with your left hand, and with a pencil in your right hand flip the curled flap quickly up and down to see how pleased your dog is!

# MORE MOVING PICTURES

You will need:

> *Eleven plain white postcards or pieces of card about the same size*
> *A pencil, and pen and ink*
> *Tracing paper*

Turn a card lengthways and make a mark with a pencil about a quarter-of-an-inch from the top. Now make another mark the same distance from the bottom, and a further one, half-an-inch from the right hand side.

On this card, draw the girl's head marked No. 1 opposite, and make sure it fits exactly inside the marks you have made. When you are satisfied you have made a good copy, trace it exactly but leave out the eyebrows and mouth. Be sure to mark on your tracing the top, bottom and sides of your card.

Now transfer the girl's head on to each card, making sure that its position is the same on all the cards. Now draw in the eyebrows and mouth on each card, changing them progressively from 1 to 6 as shown, and back again from 5 to 1. Then ink in each drawing.

Arrange the cards in a pack from 1 to 6 and back again from 5 to 1, and flick them through as shown. You will see the girl's face change from a frown to a smile and back to a frown.

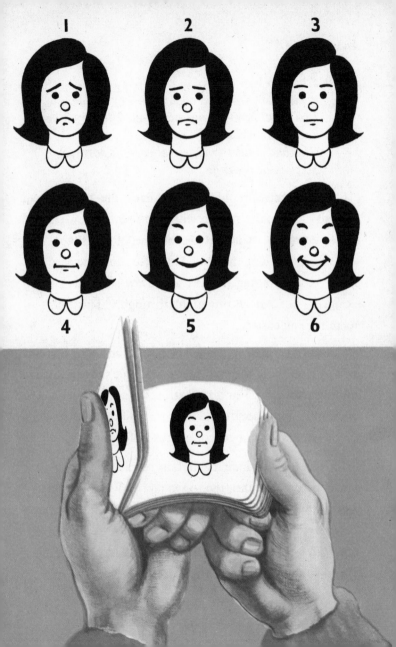

# A PERISCOPE

You will need:

> *A piece of cardboard about 9 ins. by 12½ ins.*
> *Two small handbag mirrors about 2 ins. by 3 ins.*
> *Some gummed tape*
> *Glue and a ruler (with metal edge, if possible)*
> *Scissors or penknife*

Carefully measure out on the card the plan shown opposite. An older person will help you to draw the 45° angles correctly. Cut out the outline of the shape, and score the card along the dotted lines (to score the card you place the ruler along the line and draw something sharp along it—but *not* cutting right through. This helps to make folding easier).

Cut out the small spy hole which must be about half-an-inch square. Fold the card round and glue the tabs inside, holding until dry. For added strength, add gummed tape all round. Now secure the mirrors squarely on the ends as shown, and your periscope is ready for use.

To try it out—hide behind an armchair, hold your periscope upright until the top is just above the chair and peep through the small, square hole. You will be able to see everything in the room and yet not be seen yourself. You can peep round doors, through windows and over fences—and nobody will know you are there!

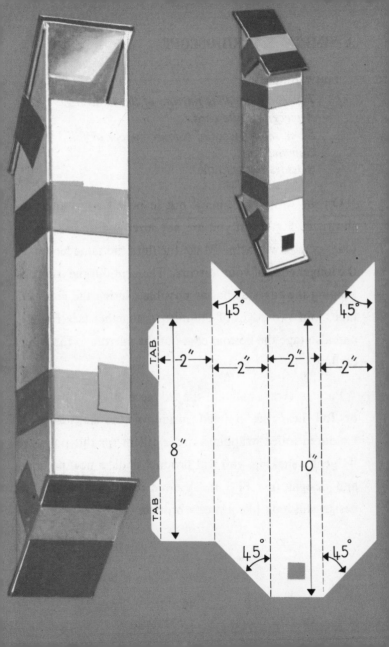

# A SIMPLE KALEIDOSCOPE

You will need:

*Two small handbag mirrors of the same size*
*A piece of white card.*
*Some small pieces of coloured paper or foil*
*Gummed tape*
*Scissors or penknife*

On the white card, mark out in pencil a 45° angle as shown in Fig. 1. If you are not sure how to do this, an older person will help. Make the lines the same length as the longer edge of your mirrors. Then cut out the triangle, keeping the edges as flat as possible. Using the gummed tape, join two edges of the mirrors together (see Fig. 2), and also tape the bottom edges of the mirrors to the white card.

Put in several small odd-shaped pieces of coloured paper or foil near the pointed inside of the kaleidoscope. Coloured toffee wrappings are excellent for this purpose. By gently shaking, you will produce endless new patterns and designs (see Fig. 3). Viewed in a bright light, the design will look like a pretty brooch.

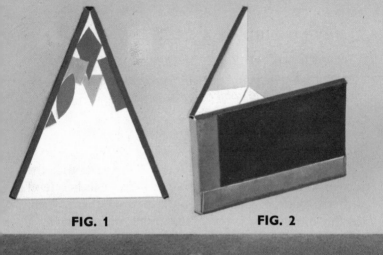

**FIG. 1**

**FIG. 2**

**FIG. 3**

# A MOVING BIRD IN A CAGE

You will need:

> *A piece of thin white card or thick paper 6 ins. by 4½ ins. and another 6 ins. by 3½ ins.*
>
> *A penknife and scissors*
>
> *A pencil and ruler*
>
> *Pen and ink*

On the larger piece of card, draw a line level with the top edge and one inch from it. Draw another level with the bottom edge and one inch from that. Then, starting one inch from the left hand side, draw a line level with the side to meet the two other lines at top and bottom. Draw another vertical line a quarter-of-an-inch from this one, and sixteen more all the same distance apart. With a sharp knife, cut the card away as shown in the picture, and you will have nine spaces and eight bars.

Now place the smaller card behind the larger, and fold half-an-inch of the top and bottom edges of the larger card back over the smaller card. The smaller card will now slide backwards and forwards easily in the grooves formed.

Place both cards flat on the table, pull the smaller card slightly to one side, and copy through the bars the shape of the bird in Fig. 1, filling in the outline in pencil right up to the bars. Then push the card slightly to the right until your drawing disappears, and draw the bird in Fig. 2, filling in the outline again. When you move the card backwards and forwards, you will find that the bird continually changes direction. If you wish, you can remove the smaller card and fill in the pencilled areas with ink.

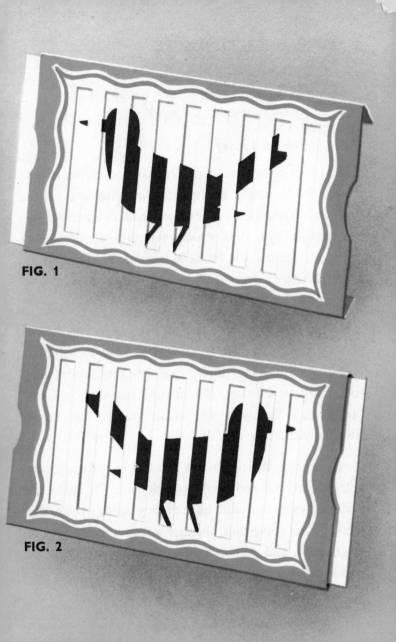

**FIG. 1**

**FIG. 2**

# A SPINNING KALEIDOSCOPE

You will need:

> *Some thin white card about 8 ins. by 8 ins.*
> *A pair of compasses and pencil*
> *Paints*
> *Scissors and string*

With your compasses, carefully draw a circle six inches across, and another a quarter-of-an-inch inside the first. Then draw a small one in the centre about one inch across. Cut out this centre hole, making sure there are no jagged edges and keeping the inside as smooth as possible. It might be better if you ask an older person to do it for you with a razor blade.

Next cut out the circle along the outer line. This can be done with scissors, but be careful to keep to the line. Divide the circle into three equal parts as shown, and colour with your paints. Be sure to match the colours in the picture as closely as you can, and to leave the narrow white border on the outside.

Pass a piece of string about two feet long through the hole, holding one end firmly in each hand. To make the disc spin, swing it around on the string once or twice, and then pull the string taut: the disc will continue to spin at great speed, and you will see a wonderful sequence of colour changes and patterns.

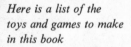

*Here is a list of the
toys and games to make
in this book*